Laughton Productions in association with Neil McPherson
for the Finborough Theatre presents the London premiere

T0353191

MERIT

by Alexandra Wood

FINBOROUGH | THEATRE

First performed at the Theatre Royal, Plymouth: 29 January 2015
First performance at the Finborough Theatre: 1 March 2016

MERIT

by Alexandra Wood

Cast in order of appearance

Sofia	**Ellie Turner**
Patricia	**Karen Ascoe**

Director	**Tom Littler**
Designer	**Philip Lindley**
Lighting Designer	**Rob Mills**
Sound Designer	**Max Pappenheim**
Producer	**Karen Ascoe**
Associate Producer	**David Upton**
Stage Manager	**Holly Marsh**

Cast and Creative Team

Karen Ascoe | Patricia

Productions at the Finborough Theatre include *Laburnum Grove.*

Trained at the Guildhall School of Music and Drama, where she won the Carleton Hobbs Award.

Theatre includes *Strangers on a Train* (English Theatre, Frankfurt); *Ashes to Ashes* (Emporium, Brighton); the title role in *Jackie The Musical* (Gardyne, Dundee); *Mansfield Park* (Theatre Royal, Bury St Edmunds, and tour); *How The Other Half Loves* (The Mill at Sonning); *Season's Greetings* (Theatre Royal Bath); *Footloose* (national tour); *Peter Pan* (Kensington Gardens); *Artefacts* (Bush and Off Broadway); *The Years Between, Adam Bede, The Case Of Rebellious Susan* (Orange Tree, Richmond); *The Letter* (Wyndham's); *Anna Karenina, After Mrs Rochester* (Shared Experience at the Lyric, Hammersmith, national and international tours); *Ivanov, Much Ado About Nothing* (Strand); *A Shayna Maidel* (Ambassadors); *Three Viewings* (New End, Hampstead); the jazz-theatre piece *Out There* (Riverside Studios); *Twelfth Night, Rookery Nook* (Mercury, Colchester); *Perfect Days, Extremities* (Derby Playhouse); *Loot, Glass Menagerie* (Swan, Worcester); *Taking Steps* and *If I Were You* (The Mill at Sonning).

Film includes *Paper Mask, Loaf* and *Daisy.*

Television includes *Drifters, My Mad Fat Diary, Cuckoo, W1A, Emmerdale, Peep Show, The Taking of Prince Harry, Casualty, Doctors, Trinity, The Bill, EastEnders, The Armando Iannucci Shows, Kid in the Corner, Armadillo* and *The Buccaneers.*

Radio includes *Tartuffe, An Ideal Husband* and *The Tempest.*

Ellie Turner | Sofia

Productions at the Finborough Theatre include *Hindle Wakes* – for which she received an Ian Charleson Award commendation – and *Drama at Inish.*

Theatre includes *Nordost* (Salisbury Playhouse and Theatre Royal Bath); *The Cherry Orchard, Hamlet* (National Theatre); *An Ideal Husband* (English Theatre, Frankfurt); *Bloody Poetry* (White Bear); *The School of Wives* for which she also received an Ian Charleson Award commendation (Upstairs at the Gatehouse); *Oliver Twist* (Riverside Studios and national tour); *Avocado* (King's Head); *La Ronde* (Riverside Studios); *The Lodger* (Arcola); *Alphabetical Order* (The Mill at Sonning); *The Playboy of the Western* (Riverside Studios and national tour) and *Henry V* (Riverside Studios and national tour).

Film includes *The Three of Us, Silence, Mother No More, Black Cab* – for which she received Best Actress in a short film at The Golden Egg Awards, New York City – and *TV Audioville*.

Television includes *Misfits*.

Alexandra Wood | Playwright

Previous plays include *The Human Ear* (Paines Plough and UK tour); *Man to Man* (Wales Millennium Centre); *Ages* (Old Vic New Voices); *The Initiate* (Paines Plough – winner of a Scotsman Fringe First); *The Empty Quarter* (Hampstead); *The Centre* (Islington Community); an adaptation of Jung Chang's *Wild Swans* (Young Vic and American Repertory Theater); *The Lion's Mouth* (Rough Cuts at the Royal Court); *The Eleventh Capital* (Royal Court) and the radio play *Twelve Years* (BBC Radio 4). She has written short plays for the Royal Court, the Oxford School of Drama, Rose Bruford College, Dry Write, Nabokov, Curious Directive and she contributed to *Decade* (Headlong). She is a past winner of the George Devine Award for Most Promising Playwright and was the Big Room Playwright-in-Residence at Paines Plough in 2013. She was formerly Literary Manager at the Finborough Theatre.

Tom Littler | Director

Productions at the Finborough Theatre include *Martine*, which achieved seven OffWestEnd Award nominations, *Jingo: A Farce of War* by Charles Wood and a season of rediscoveries comprising *The Boatswain's Mate* by Ethel Smyth, *The Mollusc* by H.H. Davies and *The Confidential Clerk* by T.S. Eliot.

Tom is Artistic Director of Primavera and Associate Director of Theatre503. Productions for Primavera include *First Episode* (Jermyn Street and Oxford); *The Living Room, Bloody Poetry, Anyone Can Whistle* (Jermyn Street); *Saturday Night* (Arts); *Origin of the Species* (Arcola); the premiere of *Shiverman* and European premiere of *Madagascar* (Theatre503); *Antigone* (Southwark Playhouse) and two seasons of *Forgotten Classics* staged readings (King's Head). Recent directing includes *Measure for Measure* (Cambridge Arts); the premiere of *Dances of Death* (Gate); *Good Grief* (Theatre Royal Bath and tour); *The Glass Menagerie, Other Desert Cities, Strangers on a Train* (English Theatre, Frankfurt); *Absurd Person Singular* (The Mill at Sonning); *Dear Liar* (Vienna's English Theatre); *The Wind in the Willows, As You Like It, Twelfth Night* (Guildford Shakespeare Company); *As You Like It* (Creation); *Tomfoolery* (UK tour); *A Little Night Music* (Menier Chocolate Factory and Central Theatre, Budapest); *Murder in the Cathedral* (Oxford Playhouse); *The Twelve-Pound Look, Mr and Mrs Nobody* and *One for the Road* (Frinton Summer).

Tom was educated at Oxford University and is studying for a Masters with the Open University. As an Assistant Director, he has worked in the West End and regionally for directors including Laurence Boswell, Peter Gill, Peter Hall, Alan Strachan and Stephen Unwin. He was Associate Director of The Peter Hall Company for three years, and worked four times as Trevor Nunn's Associate Director. Tom's work has been nominated and shortlisted multiple times for OffWestEnd Awards and has received numerous Critics' Choice Awards.

Philip Lindley | Designer

Philip is Associate Designer at the Finborough Theatre, and has designed *Mirror Teeth, Drama At Inish, Autumn Fire, The American Clock, Merrie England, The Fear of Breathing, Passing By, Somersaults, Rooms, As Is, Lost Boy* (and its subsequent transfer to Charing Cross); *The Floeurs o'Edinburgh, The Grand Tour* and *I Wish To Die Singing.*

Trained as an architect, Philip began his theatre career as a set and lighting designer before joining the BBC TV Design Department. During twenty-five years at the BBC, he worked on every type of production. The ones most remembered today include *Doctor Who, Blackadder, Top Of The Pops* and *Mastermind.* After leaving the BBC, he worked as a freelance theatre consultant before moving to Lisbon where he continued to design sets and lighting for Portuguese theatre including productions of *Cymbeline, Saturday Sunday Monday, The Bear, The Proposal, Recklessness, Tone Clusters, One For The Road, A Time For Farewells,* and *Dracula.* Since returning to the UK he has designed *Nerve* (Baron's Court); *Fair Em, Measure for Measure, Lear's Widow, Times Square Angels* (Union); *The Theban Plays* (The Scoop – *Time Out* best free London event of 2013); *Passing By* (Tristan Bates); *The Keepers Of Innocent Space* (Park); *Murderer, Blonde Bombshells of 1943* (Upstairs at the Gatehouse); *The Curing Room* (Pleasance Edinburgh and London); *The Mikado* and *Dusty* (Charing Cross).

Rob Mills | Lighting Designer

Productions at the Finborough Theatre include *I Wish to Die Singing, Obama-ology, Free as Air, Sommer 14* and *Gay's the Word.*

Theatre includes *Love Birds* (Edinburgh Festival); *Crows on the Wire* (Northern Ireland tour); *Romeo and Juliet* (Cambridge Arts); *Oedipus Retold, Making Dickie Happy* (Tristan Bates); *Tosca* (national tour and Luxembourg National Cultural Centre); *Salad Days, Biograph Girl, Daredevas* (Waterman's); *Gilbert is Dead* (Hoxton Hall); *Love Bites* (Leatherhead); *The Elixir of Love* (Stanley Hall Opera); *Napoleon Noir* (Shaw); *The Lion, the Witch and the Wardrobe, Hayton on Homicide* (Edinburgh); *Niceties* (Cambridge Footlights); *Aida* (Epsom Playhouse); *Madama Butterfly* (Harlequin); *Venus and Adonis, Dido and Aeneas, The Magic Flute* (Upstairs at the Gatehouse); *The Mikado, Yeomen of the Guard* (Minack); *Don Giovanni, Pelléas et Mélisande* (West Road Concert Hall) and *Crave* (Edinburgh Festival).

Rob has also provided the lighting and event design for a large number of live and corporate events (through his company Light Motif); ranging from the 2010 'Floating Finale' to the Lord Mayor's Show, on the River Thames, and the 2015 BAFTA TV Awards After Party.

Max Pappenheim | Sound Designer

Productions at the Finborough Theatre include *My Eyes Went Dark, I Wish to Die Singing, Coolatully, Martine, Variation on a Theme, Black Jesus, Somersaults* and *The Fear of Breathing.*

Theatre includes *Ophelias Zimmer* (Schaubühne, Berlin and Royal Court); *Jane Wenham* (Out of Joint); *Toast* (Park, national tour and 59E59 Theatres, New York); *CommonWealth* (Almeida); *Waiting for*

Godot (Sheffield Crucible); *Wink* (Theatre503); *Little Light, The Distance* (Orange Tree, Richmond); *The Glass Menagerie, Ghost, Strangers on a Train* (English Theatre, Frankfurt); *Usagi Yojimbo, Johnny Got His Gun, Three Sisters, Fiji Land, Our Ajax* (Southwark Playhouse); *Mrs Lowry and Son* (Trafalgar Studios); *The Faction's Rep Season 2015* (New Diorama); *Shopera: Carmen* (Royal Opera House, Covent Garden); *The Armour, The Hotel Plays* (Defibrillator at the Langham Hotel); *Being Tommy Cooper* (national tour); *Kafka v Kafka* (Brockley Jack) and *Awkward Conversations with Animals I've F*cked* (Underbelly, Edinburgh).

Associate Designs include *The Island* (Young Vic); *As You Like It* (Creation) and *Fleabag* (Soho).

Awards include OffWestEnd Award nominations in 2012, 2014 and 2015 for Best Sound Designer.

Holly Marsh | Stage Manager

Productions at the Finborough Theatre include *Flowering Cherry*. Trained at Northumbria University. Theatre includes *The Beauty Queen of Leenane, California Suite, The Thrill of Love, The Cripple of Inishmaan, Collaborators* and *Compleat Female Stage Beauty* (Bromley Little Theatre).

David Upton | Associate Producer

David started his working life in I.T. before moving into financial services. His love of music combined with his background in computers led to him working as a sound engineer on two acclaimed classical albums, the most recent being *Far Above the Midnight Sky.*

Production Acknowledgements

Production Photography by **Robert Workman**

Subsidised rehearsal space provided by **Jerwood Space**

Special thanks to **English Touring Theatre**, Ashley Cook, Edwin Rostron, Peter Wilkinson, Emmanuel de Lange, Sam Walters, Richard Hahlo, Nicky Blackwell and Theatre Royal, Plymouth.

FINBOROUGH | THEATRE

'A disproportionately valuable component of the London theatre ecology. Its programme combines new writing and revivals, in selections intelligent and audacious.' *Financial Times*

'The tiny but mighty Finborough... one of the best batting averages of any London company.' Ben Brantley, *The New York Times*

'The Finborough Theatre, under the artistic direction of Neil McPherson, has been earning a place on the must-visit list with its eclectic, smartly curated slate of new works and neglected masterpieces.' *Vogue*

Founded in 1980, the multi-award-winning Finborough Theatre presents plays and music theatre, concentrated exclusively on vibrant new writing and unique rediscoveries from the nineteenth and twentieth centuries. Our programme is unique – never presenting work that has been seen anywhere in London during the last twenty-five years. Behind the scenes, we continue to discover and develop a new generation of theatre makers – through our literary team, and our programmes for both interns and Resident Assistant Directors.

Despite remaining completely unsubsidised, the Finborough Theatre has an unparalleled track record of attracting the finest talent who go on to become leading voices in British theatre. Under Artistic Director Neil McPherson, it has discovered some of the UK's most exciting new playwrights including Laura Wade, James Graham, Mike Bartlett, Jack Thorne, Simon Vinnicombe, Alexandra Wood, Nicholas de Jongh and Anders Lustgarten; and directors including Blanche McIntyre, Robert Hastie and Sam Yates.

Artists working at the theatre in the 1980s included Clive Barker, Rory Bremner, Nica Burns, Kathy Burke, Ken Campbell, Jane Horrocks and Claire Dowie. In the 1990s, the Finborough Theatre first became known for new writing including Naomi Wallace's first play *The War Boys*; Rachel Weisz in David Farr's *Neville Southall's Washbag*; four plays by Anthony Neilson including *Penetrator* and *The Censor*, both of which transferred to the Royal Court Theatre; and new plays by Richard Bean, Lucinda Coxon, David Eldridge, Tony Marchant and Mark Ravenhill. New writing development included the premieres of modern classics such as Mark Ravenhill's *Shopping and F***king*, Conor McPherson's *This Lime Tree Bower*, Naomi Wallace's *Slaughter City* and Martin McDonagh's *The Pillowman*.

Since 2000, new British plays have included Laura Wade's London debut *Young Emma*, commissioned for the Finborough Theatre; two one-woman shows by Miranda Hart; James Graham's *Albert's Boy* with Victor Spinetti; Sarah Grochala's *S27*; Peter Nichols' *Lingua Franca*, which transferred Off-Broadway; Dawn King's *Foxfinder*; and West End transfers for Joy Wilkinson's *Fair*; Nicholas de Jongh's *Plague Over England*; and Jack Thorne's *Fanny and Faggot*. The late Miriam Karlin made her last stage appearance in *Many Roads to Paradise* in 2008.

We have also produced our annual festival of new writing – *Vibrant – A Festival of Finborough Playwrights* annually since 2009.

UK premieres of foreign plays have included plays by Brad Fraser, Lanford Wilson, Larry Kramer, Tennessee Williams, the English premiere of Robert McLellan's Scots language classic, *Jamie the Saxt*; and three West End transfers – Frank McGuinness' *Gates of Gold* with William Gaunt and John Bennett; Joe DiPietro's *F***ing Men*; and Craig Higginson's *Dream of the Dog* with Dame Janet Suzman.

Rediscoveries of neglected work – most commissioned by the Finborough Theatre – have included the first London revivals of Rolf Hochhuth's *Soldiers* and *The Representative*; both parts of Keith Dewhurst's *Lark Rise to Candleford*; *The Women's War*, an evening of original suffragette plays; *Etta Jenks* with Clarke Peters and Daniela Nardini; Noël Coward's first play, *The Rat Trap*; Charles Wood's *Jingo* with Susannah Harker; Emlyn Williams' *Accolade*; Lennox Robinson's *Drama at Inish* with Celia Imrie and Paul O'Grady; John Van Druten's *London Wall* which transferred to St James' Theatre; and J. B. Priestley's *Cornelius* which transferred to a sell out Off Broadway run in New York City.

Music Theatre has included the new (premieres from Grant Olding, Charles Miller, Michael John LaChuisa, Adam Guettel, Andrew Lippa, Paul Scott Goodman, and Adam Gwon's *Ordinary Days* which transferred to the West End) and the old (the UK premiere of Rodgers and Hammerstein's *State Fair* which also transferred to the West End) and the acclaimed 'Celebrating British Music Theatre' series.

The Finborough Theatre won *The Stage* Fringe Theatre of the Year Award in 2011, *London Theatre Reviews'* Empty Space Peter Brook Award in 2010 and 2012, the Empty Space Peter Brook Award's Dan Crawford Pub Theatre Award in 2005 and 2008, the Empty Space Peter Brook Mark Marvin Award in 2004, and swept the board with eight awards at the 2012 OffWestEnd Awards including Best Artistic Director and Best Director for the second year running. *Accolade* was named Best Fringe Show of 2011 by *Time Out*. It is the only unsubsidised theatre ever to be awarded the Channel 4 Playwrights Scheme nine times.

www.finboroughtheatre.co.uk

Mailing

Email admin@finboroughtheatre.co.uk or give your details to our Box Office staff to join our free email list. If you would like to be sent a free season leaflet every three months, just include your postal address and postcode.

Follow Us Online

 www.facebook.com/FinboroughTheatre

 www.twitter.com/finborough

Feedback

We welcome your comments, complaints and suggestions. Write to Finborough Theatre, 118 Finborough Road, London SW10 9ED or email us at admin@finboroughtheatre.co.uk

Playscripts

Many of the Finborough Theatre's plays have been published and are on sale from our website.

Finborough Theatre T-shirts

Finborough Theatre T-shirts are now on sale from the Box Office.

Friends

The Finborough Theatre is a registered charity. We receive no public funding, and rely solely on the support of our audiences. Please do consider supporting us by becoming a member of our Friends of the Finborough Theatre scheme. There are four categories of Friends, each offering a wide range of benefits.

Richard Tauber Friends – Val Bond. James Brown. Tom Erhardt. Stephen and Jennifer Harper. Bill Hornby. Richard Jackson. Mike Lewendon. John Lawson. Harry MacAuslan. Mark and Susan Nichols. Sarah Thomas. Kathryn McDowall. Barry Serjent. Lavinia Webb. Stephen Winningham.

Lionel Monckton Friends – Philip G Hooker. Martin and Wendy Kramer. Deborah Milner. Maxine and Eric Reynolds.

William Terriss Friends – Stuart Ffoulkes. Leo and Janet Liebster. Paul and Lindsay Kennedy. Corinne Rooney. Jon and NoraLee Sedmak.

Smoking is not permitted in the auditorium and the use of cameras and recording equipment is strictly prohibited.

In accordance with the requirements of the Royal Borough of Kensington and Chelsea:

1. The public may leave at the end of the performance by all doors and such doors must at that time be kept open.
2. All gangways, corridors, staircases and external passageways intended for exit shall be left entirely free from obstruction whether permanent or temporary.
3. Persons shall not be permitted to stand or sit in any of the gangways intercepting the seating or to sit in any of the other gangways.

The Finborough Theatre is licensed by the Royal Borough of Kensington and Chelsea to The Steam Industry, a registered charity and a company limited by guarantee. Registered in England and Wales no. 3448268. Registered Charity no. 1071304. Registered Office: 118 Finborough Road, London SW10 9ED. The Steam Industry is under the overall Artistic Direction of Phil Willmott.
www.philwillmott.co.uk

MERIT

Alexandra Wood

Merit was first performed at the Theatre Royal Plymouth on
29 January 2015, with the following cast:

PATRICIA   Rebecca Lacey
SOFIA   Lizzy Watts

Director   Jennie Darnell
Set and Costume Designer   Matthew Wright
Lighting and Projection Designer Jason Taylor
Sound Designer   Adrienne Quartly
Casting Director   Stephen Moore
Assistant Director   Phil Bartlett

For Helen and Kieron Cooke

Thanks

I'd like to thank Richard Twyman, Vanessa Montfort, Nadia Clifford, Meera Syal and Paul Chahidi, for their involvement in the original short play, written as part of *PIIGS* at the Royal Court; George Perrin, James Grieve and the anonymous playwright who made it possible for me to spend time in residence at Paines Plough, where I wrote the play; Lu Kemp, Lizzy Watts and Sandy McDade, who allowed me to hear it for the first time; Lisa, my agent; David Prescott and Simon Stokes at Theatre Royal Plymouth for giving it a home; Jennie Darnell and the brilliant cast and production team for bringing it to life.

A.W.

'It's hard to go through life without killing someone.'

Canada, Richard Ford

Characters

PATRICIA, *fifty*
SOFIA, *twenty-three, her daughter*

Note on Text

A forward slash (/) in the text indicates a point of interruption.

A lack of punctuation at the end of the line indicates that the speaker cannot or does not want to continue.

One

SOFIA. Most parents would be happy, given the way things are, given the current / situation

PATRICIA. I am. We are Sofia.

SOFIA. Most parents would be fucking ecstatic in fact.

PATRICIA. No need to swear, is / there?

SOFIA. Down on their knees.

PATRICIA. You think we should be down on / our

SOFIA. Giving thanks that their child, their beloved, so-called beloved child

PATRICIA. Of course you're loved, that's not / in question.

SOFIA. Has got work. Is in a job. Can provide the family with some relief, so I'm sorry if that's / not the case

PATRICIA. And why is that?

SOFIA. What?

PATRICIA. Why are they down on their knees?

SOFIA. What do you mean, why do you think, because

PATRICIA. Because jobs are scarce.

SOFIA. There are no jobs, so if their child is lucky enough to / have

PATRICIA. Luck?

SOFIA. More than half of us aren't in work. We graduate and there's nothing so when someone manages to get one of the precious few jobs out there that still pays a decent, yes, their families are down on their knees.

I manage to get one of these, against all the odds, against all the thousands of overqualified, over-educated candidates / and I'm

PATRICIA. That's just it.

SOFIA. What is?

PATRICIA. We're worried

SOFIA. We?

PATRICIA. Your father and I. We need to know, we really would feel better knowing that you're not

That this job

SOFIA. Yes?

PATRICIA. That it's not costing you, more than it's

SOFIA. Costing me? It doesn't cost me anything. They pay me, that's how it works Mum.

PATRICIA. Please don't patronise me / Sofia.

SOFIA. Unless you're talking about, what are you talking about my soul? You're worried about my soul? Because I work for, you're worried about my eternal

We haven't been to church in twenty years, we don't even go at Christmas, and now all of / a sudden

PATRICIA. That's not really

SOFIA. It's a good job.

PATRICIA. We do go sometimes.

No one's denying that it's a good job. Extremely well paid, I mean, you're already earning far more than your father so

SOFIA. Job of my dreams.

PATRICIA. And we're happy for you.

SOFIA. Are you?

PATRICIA. Of course we're

There's no need to get all

SOFIA. In my field I couldn't really do much better, PA to a politician maybe, but in these times it's not the politicians running things, so actually

And I enjoy it. Is that wrong?

PATRICIA. Of course not.

SOFIA. I love that I'm the only one who can make out Antonio's handwriting. He's had to dictate things before, but by some miracle I can read it. He relies on me and I love it.

PATRICIA. You call him by his first name.

SOFIA. Everyone / does.

PATRICIA. That's very

SOFIA. Why shouldn't I?

PATRICIA. Pay packet like that. Straight out of university. No experience.

We're in no doubt that it's a good job.

SOFIA. Right, well I'm so pleased we've established / that.

PATRICIA. And look, times like these, people can't afford to be high and mighty about who's paying their wages.

SOFIA. They're lucky to have wages.

I marched, didn't I? I don't like the situation, the way things are.

Clara barely speaks to me now, and she's not busy, what could she possibly be doing, so I can only imagine it's jealousy, and I don't want to think that, she's my oldest friend, we've done everything together our whole lives, but I think this has come between us, and that makes me sad, but I haven't done anything wrong, and I will not apologise for having a job, I won't do that.

PATRICIA. Has anyone asked you to?

SOFIA. It feels like that's where this is

We marched for jobs, so what kind of sense does it make to resent those people lucky enough to have one?

PATRICIA. Luck?

SOFIA. Yes, luck, Mum. I've never claimed to be the smartest person in the world, I've got no illusions about my academic ability. I'm average, I accept that.

PATRICIA. Don't say that Sofia.

SOFIA. It's true, but that's okay, and it hasn't stopped me. I work hard and the fact is, I'm employed, Antonio saw something in me and gave me the job. That's not my fault.

PATRICIA. He saw something in you?

SOFIA. God knows he had his pick of candidates, so yeah, I guess he saw something in me. Is that hard for you to believe, as my mother, do you find that so hard to believe?

PATRICIA. It's just, you said yourself Sofia, you said yourself, you probably weren't the best-qualified candidate, fine, it's not all about academic qualifications.

But it's not like you have any work experience either.

SOFIA. Is that my fault?

PATRICIA. No, and if it was me, of course I'd hire you in a flash, you've got so much to give, I know that, but I'm your mother and

SOFIA. And what?

PATRICIA. He's not.

He's just a man. Who had his pick of these candidates, most of whom, I assume, given the nature of the, were women, I think it's probably fair to assume that.

You said he saw something in you. What did he see?

SOFIA. My inner brilliance.

I don't know what he saw, what kind of question is that?

PATRICIA. What did you show him then?

SOFIA. What did I

Fuck.

You think I offered him things, don't you?

PATRICIA. I just want to be clear.

SOFIA. Sex. My body. You think I prostituted myself for a job.

You don't think I'm capable of impressing someone sufficiently with my professionalism and personality. You think I had to offer him sex.

What do you imagine, that I did a Sharon Stone, that I showed him everything on offer?

Do you know me at all?

PATRICIA. I love you Sofia.

SOFIA. What's that got to do with it, you think I'm a whore, essentially, you're accusing me of sleeping my way into a job, my own mother.

PATRICIA. These are desperate times. I know you'd never do anything like that in a / normal

SOFIA. Don't hear you complain when I pay the electricity bill.

PATRICIA. Don't be like that.

SOFIA. Don't hear you complain when I buy your groceries at the end of the month.

PATRICIA. We're grateful darling, that's not what's in question.

SOFIA. No, what's in question, apparently, is my integrity.

PATRICIA. People can sometimes feel they have no choice and your father and I, we just want you to know that you do have a choice.

SOFIA. What is it?

PATRICIA. Some things are more valuable than a job.

SOFIA. Like my vagina?

PATRICIA. If you're going to be crude

SOFIA. Crude? You just accused me of being a whore.

Pause.

PATRICIA. When you become a parent, Sofia, a mother, there are certain things you want your child to know, that you want them to value and, soul is a loaded term but I suppose, / yes

SOFIA. I have had sex.

PATRICIA. That's not

Sex is fine, of course it is, but sex in exchange for a job or a

SOFIA. That's not fine?

PATRICIA. You're worth more than that Sofia, please tell me you're not

SOFIA. Please tell me you're not actually asking.

But you are.

Antonio's a good man. / Just because

PATRICIA. He's a powerful man.

SOFIA. Just because he earns a lot, doesn't make him some kind of predatory monster, some / rapacious

PATRICIA. Well actually darling, that is what they are.

SOFIA. Can you hear yourself?

PATRICIA. People like him, they're used to a certain way of thinking, Sofia, they're used to taking whatever they want and getting away with it, they're not used to being told no, they're / not used to

SOFIA. He's married.

PATRICIA. Please, that's hardly

SOFIA. He's got three kids.

PATRICIA. Why not? He can afford them.

SOFIA. I don't have to defend him, or myself, what am I doing? If you don't want my money, fine, but don't come crying to me

PATRICIA. Don't be like that.

We love you Sofia.

SOFIA. You obviously don't think I'm worth very much at all
Mum, if you find it so hard to / believe

PATRICIA. Don't say that, / it's not true.

SOFIA. that I could get a job on actual merit.

PATRICIA. Please Sofia.

Pause.

You still haven't denied it, you still haven't said,
categorically, that you haven't

SOFIA. You'd have lost the house. Without my devil money
you'd be on the street, you wouldn't be eating in restaurants,
it'd be lentil stew, or whatever you're given. Without my job
we certainly wouldn't be going to Daniel's wedding in the
Canaries, there'd be nothing, nothing to look forward to. But
I'll quit, shall I? I'll join the millions of unemployed, where I
belong apparently, according to my mother.

PATRICIA. You're still not denying it.

SOFIA. Am I supposed to make it easier for you to accept my
money? Reassure you I've done nothing immoral, nothing
shameful to earn it? Is that what you want out of this?

PATRICIA. Why not Clara?

Why not Daniel? Why not the Hernandez boys? Always top
of the class. Why you and not them?

SOFIA. I don't know.

Of course they should have jobs. Of course they deserve
them as much as me. Of course they'd work as hard, of
course they're as smart, as good with people, as everything
as me, if not better, so I don't know why me and not them
Mum.

But I work hard.

PATRICIA. That's not what's in question.

SOFIA. I'm talented, aren't I?

PATRICIA *nods.*

So maybe, despite my lack of experience and my average intellectual capabilities, maybe Antonio saw something in me, is that really so hard to believe?

PATRICIA *shakes her head.*

I'll tell you what is hard to believe, heartbreakingly hard to believe, that he can see something in me that you can't. Some potential, some spark, some germ of, I don't know, something, and you know what, that's why he earns the big bucks and you don't. The weak and the unimaginative want to blame him for their problems, but all he does is see potential in things. He dares to take a risk. He doesn't think things ordinary people like you think, that she's an unknown quantity, I'll play it safe, that doesn't even cross his mind, he has the courage of his convictions and he goes for it. He saw something in me, and who are you, who are you to say there's nothing there? That all he saw was a quick blow job. An easy fuck.

PATRICIA. That's not what I

SOFIA. Maybe I'm not like you, maybe that's what he saw.

PATRICIA. Don't say that Sofia, you're my daughter, of course you're like me.

Two

SOFIA. What're you doing here?

PATRICIA. I wanted to see my daughter. Haven't seen you in

SOFIA. Whose fault's that?

PATRICIA. Please Sofia, can we be kind?

SOFIA. Kind?

PATRICIA. Please.

SOFIA. I can be kind.

PATRICIA. I know you can.

You're angry, I understand that, you were offended.

SOFIA. Most people would've been.

PATRICIA. I'm sorry for that. I never meant to

SOFIA. My mistake.

Pause.

PATRICIA. We haven't bothered you. We've let you be. At Clara's.

How is Clara?

SOFIA. No job.

PATRICIA. I don't understand it.

SOFIA. I did try to help her.

PATRICIA. You're a kind friend.

Are you still on the sofa?

SOFIA. It's a sofa bed.

PATRICIA. And they're taking your money for that?

SOFIA. I offered.

PATRICIA. Doesn't seem right, doesn't seem fair.

SOFIA. It helps them.

PATRICIA. Them?

Good, well. I hope it's comfortable at least?

SOFIA. Comfortable enough.

PATRICIA. How's work?

SOFIA *nods*.

Your boss / still

SOFIA. Antonio.

PATRICIA. Antonio still

SOFIA. What? A banker?

PATRICIA. You're still getting on?

SOFIA. Yes thank you.

PATRICIA. Was that him you were with?

SOFIA *shakes her head.*

Another colleague. Looked nice.

SOFIA. He's not really.

PATRICIA. Oh. Well.

SOFIA. Is that my jacket?

PATRICIA. You left it behind, I assumed it wasn't one of your favourites, but I didn't have anything appropriate.

SOFIA. For what? Standing outside an office. There's no dress code Mum.

PATRICIA. Well I was hoping to, that I might, that you might be able to give me a tour.

SOFIA. A tour?

PATRICIA. It's a lovely building, I'm sure it's very impressive inside.

SOFIA. Just an office.

PATRICIA. You're blasé already, look at it Sofia, it's very nice.

SOFIA. Didn't know you're interested in architecture.

PATRICIA. It's where you work, where my daughter works, forgive me if I'm interested.

SOFIA. Surprised you want to go inside. It's full of bankers.

PATRICIA. Oh come on Sofia, I'm not

SOFIA. Might catch something.

PATRICIA. Sofia.

SOFIA. They take what they want Mum, I couldn't protect you.

PATRICIA. I'm sorry. What I said, it was silly, it was

Pause.

I'd love to see where you work. Your desk, your space.

SOFIA. It's been a long day.

PATRICIA. Is Antonio still up there? I'd love to meet him, see what all the fuss is about.

SOFIA. He's on a conference call.

PATRICIA. Oh.

SOFIA. Anyway, you can't just waltz in without an appointment, you'd need a pass.

PATRICIA. I'd be with you.

SOFIA. You'd need a pass.

PATRICIA. I just want a look around, what do they think I'm going to do?

SOFIA. Some people hate us, as you well know.

PATRICIA. I'm your mother.

SOFIA. They don't care.

PATRICIA. Wouldn't touch anything.

SOFIA. Look if it matters that much to you, I'll organise a tour another day, but not now, I'm exhausted.

PATRICIA. It's late.

SOFIA. How long've you been waiting here?

PATRICIA. Not long, since five.

SOFIA. It's nine thirty.

PATRICIA. I didn't know when you finished, I didn't / know.

SOFIA. I never finish at five.

Were you just going to hang around, I might not have even been in.

PATRICIA. Where else would you be?

SOFIA. What are you doing here?

PATRICIA. You refused to return my calls. What choice did I have?

SOFIA. What's so urgent?

PATRICIA. I wanted to see my daughter.

SOFIA. Stop saying 'my daughter', I know we're related, you don't have to keep stating it like it's in doubt.

PATRICIA. I'm sorry. You. I wanted to see you.

SOFIA. Well here I am. Tired and hungry.

Do you want to get some food?

I'll buy you dinner.

PATRICIA. You don't have to buy me dinner Sofia.

SOFIA. Fine, you pay, either way, I need to eat.

PATRICIA. How long will Antonio's conference call be? Perhaps he could join us.

SOFIA. I doubt he'd

He'll head home.

PATRICIA. Just a quick drink. Don't tell me he always rushes straight home, I know how it works.

SOFIA. He does, actually. Why the sudden interest?

PATRICIA. This man, he gave my daughter, sorry, you, he gave you a chance, and you spend your working week together, is it strange I'd like to meet him?

SOFIA. Last time we spoke you thought he was a sexual predator.

PATRICIA. That's not true.

SOFIA. A rapacious banker, corrupt, corrupting, you thought he would steal my soul, so yes, Mum, it's a bit of a turnaround.

PATRICIA. You put me right.

If you respect him the way you do, if you think highly of him, then I trust that. I trust your judgement.

SOFIA. Isn't my judgement marred by the bewitching power and wealth of these evil bankers?

PATRICIA. Look it's nothing to worry about but your father lost his job.

SOFIA. What? When?

PATRICIA. A week or two ago.

I've tried calling but you weren't responding so

SOFIA. He's been there years, they can't just

PATRICIA. He finishes up at the end of the week.

SOFIA. Just like that?

PATRICIA. He'll get some severance pay.

What can they do?

SOFIA. How is he?

PATRICIA. Who knows, maybe it's a good thing.

SOFIA. How? How could it be a good thing?

PATRICIA. Maybe it's an opportunity for me to do something.

SOFIA. What?

PATRICIA. I've got skills, Sofia, life experience, I've got plenty to offer.

SOFIA. Now's hardly the time to be

If Clara can't find anything then

PATRICIA. You found something.

We're not so different are we?

SOFIA. What are you thinking of doing?

PATRICIA. Well it'll have to be something with a decent salary, but I'm not precious, I'd consider most things.

SOFIA. Like what?

PATRICIA. I have worked before Sofia.

SOFIA. I'm not sure you quite appreciate what it's like now.

PATRICIA. I appreciate it just fine, thank you.

You've got to put yourself out there. Clara's always been a quiet girl, and that's all well and good, but you got it right.

SOFIA. Put yourself out there?

PATRICIA. You're a go-getter Sofia, but where d'you think you get that?

SOFIA. I don't know.

PATRICIA. I really would like to speak to Antonio, when will his call be done do you think?

SOFIA. Why now?

PATRICIA. No time like the present.

SOFIA. What's going on? Why are you wearing my jacket?

PATRICIA. Have to look presentable, and I didn't have anything suitable, it's been a long time since I've worked in an office.

SOFIA. You want to work here?

PATRICIA. Why not? What's alright for my daughter, you, what's good for you, is more than good enough for me.

SOFIA. And you think you can just walk into a job here?

PATRICIA. I appreciate how competitive it is, but

SOFIA. I don't think you do.

What's the plan, meet Antonio, wear the right clothes, convince him the bank can't go on without you?

PATRICIA. It's a start.

SOFIA. Because it's that easy.

PATRICIA. It's a start, that's all I'm talking about.

SOFIA. You didn't want to see me, you wanted to see Antonio.

PATRICIA. I'd see you every day if I could Sofia. If it was up to me, you'd be back at home where you belong. Not paying to sleep on a sofa.

SOFIA. You miss the money. My rent, that's what you miss.

PATRICIA. We miss you.

I haven't come asking for a handout, have I? I'm not here for that. I'm very happy to go out and work.

SOFIA. You've got no idea.

PATRICIA. It makes sense to start looking somewhere you have an in, somewhere they know you.

SOFIA. Antonio doesn't know you.

PATRICIA. He knows you. Look, I'm not talking about anything underhand.

SOFIA. So you're not planning to offer him sex then?

PATRICIA. I won't embarrass you.

SOFIA. So what exactly do you plan to offer?

PATRICIA. You said you'd be kind.

SOFIA. I am being kind, I'm trying to tell you, Mum, you have no idea. If you go in there begging for a job it'll be excruciating.

PATRICIA. I never said beg.

SOFIA. Excruciating Mum.

PATRICIA. You don't think he'll shake my hand and be polite?

If he's the man you say he is, won't he ask me questions, nod and smile politely at my answers, even if he has no intention of employing me, won't he do that at the very least?

What's excruciating about that?

SOFIA. There is no job, I don't know what you / think

PATRICIA. It doesn't have to be at the bank. Perhaps he needs someone to look after the children, you said he has children.

SOFIA. A nanny?

PATRICIA. I just about managed not to kill you, I could look after children.

SOFIA. His wife's at home, he doesn't need a / nanny.

PATRICIA. These are just examples, Sofia. He'll have friends, if he's the man you say he is, he must have friends, contacts, people he knows. I fail to believe that I couldn't be of use to at least one of them, in some capacity.

SOFIA. I'm hungry Mum, can we talk about this over dinner?

PATRICIA. I'd rather see him first.

SOFIA. I told you he's / busy.

PATRICIA. Your father finishes in four days' time Sofia. Four days between us and nothing. So I don't intend to waste a minute. I'm here now, he's up there, the call will have to end at some point, what's the harm in having a quick chat to me afterwards, is it really going to hurt, is it really going to be so excruciating?

SOFIA. It's nine thirty, he's had a long day, he's probably hungry, wants to get home, you think he'll be in the mood right now?

PATRICIA. When else?

SOFIA. I'll ask him, if it means that much to you, I'll ask him if he'd mind.

PATRICIA. You say he helps people, gives a quarter of his money away, some kind of altruist, so surely he won't mind having a simple chat with me?

PATRICIA *sits*.

SOFIA. What're you doing?

PATRICIA. I'll wait.

SOFIA. You can't wait here, what's wrong with you?

PATRICIA. Why not? I've been here four and a half hours already and nothing terrible's happened.

I might catch him on his way out.

SOFIA. I said I'd ask him for you didn't I?

PATRICIA. And I'm sure you will, but I might be able to save you the trouble.

SOFIA. Let's get some food.

PATRICIA. If I'm to eat, Sofia, if your father and I are to eat in the future, I need to wait right here.

SOFIA. Don't be ridiculous.

PATRICIA. Is it ridiculous?

Four days. Four.

SOFIA. As if I'd leave you on the street. To starve, on the street.

PATRICIA. I'll be fine here. Go and get your dinner.

SOFIA. I'm not leaving you here.

PATRICIA. What do you think's going to happen? We're in the middle of a city, there are guards right through there, street lights, what's going to happen?

SOFIA. He could be hours.

PATRICIA. I've got nowhere to be.

Pause.

SOFIA. I'll call him.

He might have ten minutes tomorrow. If I can get you ten minutes, will you go home now?

PATRICIA. I'm not hurting anyone sitting here, am I?

SOFIA. It's getting cold.

PATRICIA. I've got my coat.

SOFIA. Why can't you just apply for some jobs online? Go to the Jobcentre. Like normal people.

PATRICIA. What would that achieve? Like you said, if Clara can't get anything then

No, this is what it takes Sofia.

SOFIA. I'll ask him, okay, I'll ask if he'd mind, ten minutes, when he's finished, that's all, okay, he's got to get home.

PATRICIA. Ten minutes, that's all.

Three

SOFIA. You know where I'm staying, I don't know why you can't go there, why you have to loiter outside the office like a

PATRICIA. Like a?

SOFIA. Are you trying to see Antonio again, is that it?

I tried telling you there'd be nothing he could do.

PATRICIA. It was very good of him to meet me.

SOFIA. It's hardly standard practice, meeting the parents, it's not required, he did it / as a

PATRICIA. I'm not here to see him.

SOFIA. If it's me you want to see, we can arrange to meet somewhere, or come to Clara's but don't just hang around waiting for

Nina and Cristos are always saying it'd be nice to see you.

PATRICIA. Are you still on the sofa?

SOFIA. Sofa bed.

PATRICIA. You must be starting to feel in the way, can't be easy living in other people's space.

SOFIA. I'm hardly there.

PATRICIA. Have to get used to it I suppose.

SOFIA. They're like family anyway so

PATRICIA. They're not family Sofia.

SOFIA. Like. I said like. We've known each other our whole lives. I know they're not family but

PATRICIA. Your security guards have guns, did you know that?

SOFIA. Of course they do.

PATRICIA. Of course?

SOFIA. Well how else are they going to

It's a deterrent.

PATRICIA. I suddenly thought, in my duffel coat, they might think I'm concealing something.

SOFIA. It's cold, they're not going to shoot you for wearing a duffel coat.

PATRICIA. You hear stories.

SOFIA. What stories?

PATRICIA. I wrote you a letter.

SOFIA. A letter?

PATRICIA. We stopped the internet and the phone, we don't need them.

SOFIA. I didn't get it.

PATRICIA. I didn't send it, in the end.

SOFIA. What did it say?

PATRICIA. The point is, I'm not running to you at the first sign of

I've been trying, speaking to people, putting myself out there, Antonio was just one of many I've, one of Guido's colleagues, I spoke to him, so there's every chance, these things take time, but I could get an interview tomorrow, any time, but

Until then, until that time, we're not going to be able to pay the mortgage, in fact, we're going to

We're going to

The house. We'll lose the house.

Without your help Sofia.

Look I'm sorry to do this here, but I didn't want to go to Clara's. I know you've been friends a long time, but we're your family Sofia, not them.

I was surprised when you told us you were moving in there anyway, after what you'd said, how things were tense between you, because of the job.

SOFIA. At least she never questioned how I got it.

PATRICIA. This is the family home we're talking about, Sofia, our home, the roof over our heads, you can't possibly risk that for the sake of some petty misunderstanding.

SOFIA. It wasn't a misunderstanding.

PATRICIA. Did you hear me Sofia? We'll lose the house.

SOFIA *nods*.

We've been cutting back, we've tried, and we fully intend to get back to work as soon as possible, but until then

SOFIA. There are a billion people, including us, who live better now than kings and queens did in the past.

PATRICIA. You name a king or queen who struggled to pay the mortgage on a two-bedroom house.

SOFIA. We enjoy unimaginable levels of comfort and security.

PATRICIA. Security? I just told you we'll lose the house Sofia. We'll be on a sofa next.

SOFIA. There are worse things Mum.

PATRICIA. Maybe it's fun for you, in your twenties, maybe it's all one big adventure but your father and I haven't been working our whole lives to end up on some sofa.

SOFIA. We're the lucky ones, we have responsibilities and actually, we can do far more than we think.

PATRICIA. Is this Antonio talking again?

SOFIA. If I sleep on Clara's sofa bed, save my money, give everything I can, I could really help people, Mum.

PATRICIA. Your father tried to kill himself.

SOFIA. He tried to

What?

When? When did this happen?

PATRICIA. A week

SOFIA. And you didn't think to tell me? Immediately, your daughter, his daughter, you didn't think I should know?

PATRICIA. He's fine now.

SOFIA. He tried to kill himself Mum and you didn't think that was worth a phone call?

PATRICIA. I knew he'd be okay.

SOFIA. Who did you call? A friend? / A

PATRICIA. No one.

SOFIA. So you want to suffer in silence, store it up and hit me with it, without so much as a warning, without a

PATRICIA. Listen, he doesn't know I've told you. You can't ever talk about it with him.

SOFIA. So you finally get round to telling me and I'm supposed to ignore it? Forget I know?

PATRICIA. You don't have to forget you know, you just can't say anything. It'd kill him.

SOFIA. Why would he

PATRICIA. We're about to lose the house and you ask why.

SOFIA. It's a house, Mum, it's not worth

Not Dad, no, Dad just gets on and fixes things. Leaking taps. Punctured tyres. He's not one to get

PATRICIA. He's not the only one.

There are plenty of people now, on the news all the time, the figures, people lose all hope and can't see a better option.

SOFIA. He's lost all hope?

PATRICIA. Well it looked like that when I found him.

No, look he hasn't lost all

SOFIA. How did he

PATRICIA. Pills.

SOFIA. What pills?

PATRICIA. Paracetamol. Household stuff, nothing fancy.

SOFIA. Did they pump his stomach?

PATRICIA *shakes her head.*

So what, he didn't take enough or what?

PATRICIA. I guess not.

SOFIA. So maybe it was just a cry for help?

PATRICIA. Possibly.

SOFIA. Well what did the doctors say?

PATRICIA. We didn't go to the hospital. There was no need.

SOFIA. No need? He tried to kill himself.

PATRICIA. I found him in time.

SOFIA. He could have blood poisoning. And don't you think he might need some help, psychological, at least counselling or something.

PATRICIA. He's got me.

SOFIA. You're not

You have to take him to a doctor Mum.

PATRICIA. Those kinds of doctors are expensive.

SOFIA. I'll pay. He needs to get checked over at least, the drugs might have done damage, you don't know.

PATRICIA. He's much better.

SOFIA. If he's lost all hope

That doesn't just go away, that stays with you, he could try again, where is he now?

PATRICIA. He's at home.

SOFIA. Alone?

PATRICIA. He's not a child.

SOFIA. Is he alone Mum?

PATRICIA. Guido's with him.

SOFIA. Oh, great, 'cause he's a barrel of laughs. Really uplifting little anecdotes he tells.

PATRICIA. He's not going to kill himself over one of Guido's stories.

SOFIA. It could tip him over the edge.

PATRICIA. Don't be extreme.

SOFIA. Well what did? There must've been a trigger, something to push him, something / that made

PATRICIA. Take your pick Sofia, hardly a shortage of

It's not difficult, is it, to see why someone might lose hope.

SOFIA. Not Dad.

PATRICIA. Why not? He can see what's happening, where this is all going.

SOFIA. We're luckier than most.

PATRICIA. We?

SOFIA. You, me, Dad.

PATRICIA. Perhaps he doesn't feel like there is a 'we'.

Pause.

SOFIA. You think me leaving, you think that's what pushed him, what got to him?

PATRICIA. I think it doesn't have to be any one thing.

SOFIA. But you think it's one of the things.

Pause.

Why wasn't it the first thing you said to me?

Don't you think, don't you think it's significant news, worth mentioning straight off?

PATRICIA. What, hello Sofia, your father tried to kill himself.

You would've preferred that greeting?

SOFIA. Yes, actually.

PATRICIA. Well I'll know for next time.

SOFIA. How can

How can you even attempt a joke?

PATRICIA. I didn't know if I'd tell you. That's why I didn't run up to you weeping and wailing. He didn't want me to, and I wasn't sure.

SOFIA. But you did.

PATRICIA. Yes.

SOFIA. Why?

Pause.

PATRICIA. Are you going to help us?

SOFIA. Don't you think it could happen again?

PATRICIA. It won't.

SOFIA. And you're sure of that are you? He's fixed. Just like that. Brief brush with death's enough to solve all his problems.

PATRICIA. You could do that. You're in a position to solve his

SOFIA. A thousand a month or whatever the mortgage is, that's all it'd take?

PATRICIA. Yes.

SOFIA. Is that how it works?

PATRICIA. That's the difference between losing your home and keeping it so yes, that's enough to

That's what Antonio would say, isn't it? Throw money at the problem. What he does, why he gives away a quarter of his salary.

SOFIA. It's not the same at all, his money goes towards health schemes, vaccines, practical things, they need money to fund the most basic / things.

PATRICIA. Shelter, that's one of the basics isn't it? Well this is our shelter.

You want to save lives, well start with your father's.

SOFIA. How can I say no to that?

PATRICIA. Do you want to say no?

Pause.

SOFIA. If I come back, I want Dad to speak to someone, at least.

PATRICIA. There's no need for that if you're helping us.

SOFIA. No, no, if I come back, I want to know Dad's getting help.

PATRICIA. You can't force someone, Sofia, you can't force him to talk to a stranger about private

Look it was just a moment of desperation, that's all.

Come home. That's all he needs.

Four

PATRICIA. It's his wedding, you only get one of those.

SOFIA. If it was down the road of course we'd be there Mum, but it's not, it's three return flights, it's hotels for at least a couple of nights.

PATRICIA. A week, we'd go for at least / a week.

SOFIA. What's that going to come to? Two grand?

PATRICIA. It's his wedding.

SOFIA. We can't afford it.

PATRICIA. Your father and I have been looking forward to this for a year, and now, a few weeks before, in the homeware department, in the middle of buying their present, you tell me no.

SOFIA. You can still buy them a present.

PATRICIA. I want to watch them open it Sofia, I want to be there to see them open it.

SOFIA. I'm just trying to be realistic.

PATRICIA. This is what Dad needs.

Don't you think a joyful, family occasion, some time away from here, is just what the doctor ordered?

SOFIA. If he'd seen one.

PATRICIA. You can't take that away from him. Us. You can't do that.

SOFIA. You're not children Mum, he's not a child, we can't afford it, simple, what do you want me to say?

PATRICIA. Can we afford these wine glasses or are they too extravagant as well?

SOFIA. You might want to get something easier to send.

PATRICIA. You're enjoying this.

SOFIA. Why would I enjoy it? I wanted to go. Daniel's the closest thing I've got to a brother, of course I want to be at his wedding, and if it was just me then

PATRICIA. What?

SOFIA. It's just not sensible to be spending that much / on

PATRICIA. If it was just you, you'd go.

SOFIA. I can't afford to now but

I was looking forward to going, so don't make out like this is fun for me. Cancelling. Like that's fun.

PATRICIA. There are some things in life, Sofia, you just have to find a way.

SOFIA. I don't think holidays count as the bare essentials Mum.

PATRICIA. Weddings, funerals, big things. You just find a way to be there.

SOFIA. Go ahead then, find a way.

If you've got some rich friend who'll lend us the money, or some secret stash I don't / know about.

PATRICIA. You're the one with the rich friends.

SOFIA. Hardly.

PATRICIA. Antonio.

SOFIA. He's my boss.

PATRICIA. You're friends as well aren't you?

SOFIA. I'm not asking him for

Look, I want to go, but I can accept that it's not possible this time.

PATRICIA. This time? There is no other time Sofia, this is it. One time only.

It's obviously just not as important to you, family.

SOFIA. No, family means nothing to me, does it, I mean I haven't supported you and Dad in any way have I so

PATRICIA. I'm not missing his day. What would Tomas have said?

SOFIA. Uncle Tomas was always a reasonable man.

He would've understood. Just as Daniel does.

PATRICIA. So you've already told him? You've already

Without even talking to me.

SOFIA. I'm talking to you now.

PATRICIA. In the middle of / the

SOFIA. Dad's always at home and I wanted to

I wanted to speak to you first.

PATRICIA. Well you can tell your father, I'm not doing that.

Pause.

SOFIA. We'll go another time. When everything's more settled.

PATRICIA. When will that be?

Pause.

Are you giving your money away?

SOFIA. Mum

PATRICIA. You are, aren't you?

SOFIA. I've taken over the mortgage, I'm doing my bit.

PATRICIA. Like Antonio, you're giving it away.

SOFIA. That's not your concern Mum.

PATRICIA. It is when I miss my only nephew's wedding.

Antonio can afford to give his money away, that's nice he's got so much to spare. You don't earn anything like as much as him, you can't be expected / to

SOFIA. There are things happening in the rest of the world. Worse than missing a wedding. Terrible, preventable, things. So yes, I will give, even if it means missing out now and again, I don't have to explain my choices to you.

Pause.

PATRICIA. I am still

I am still trying to find something.

Antonio never got back to me. Such a great man, but he can't manage simple manners.

SOFIA. What's he supposed to say?

PATRICIA. He said he'd let me know if anything came up, anything suitable.

SOFIA. Then I guess it hasn't.

PATRICIA. What could I do, anyway.

SOFIA. It's not a personal slight, Mum, he can't just conjure a job out of thin air.

PATRICIA. Obviously he didn't see anything in me. Whatever he saw in you, apparently I don't have it.

Or it disappeared with age, who knows.

Pause.

How does he justify it? Antonio. All this fuss about other people, elsewhere, helping them, but what about us? Here. On his doorstep.

SOFIA. I don't know why you've got it in for Antonio. At least he tries to do something to help, he's not blind to the fact there are problems, he's not living in a bubble.

PATRICIA. Where does he live?

SOFIA. That's not fair.

PATRICIA. He's not on someone's sofa is he. He has a house, a garden, a pool, probably.

SOFIA. So?

PATRICIA. Where does he live?

SOFIA. I don't know, I've never been to his house.

PATRICIA. He's never mentioned it, the area, it's never come up in conversation?

SOFIA. Okay, he probably has a nice house.

PATRICIA. Couple, probably.

SOFIA. Does it matter?

PATRICIA. Yes, because it's a lie isn't it, all this giving, all this altruistic bullshit, because he keeps enough for himself, him and his family, they're fine.

SOFIA. Okay so he's not Mother Teresa, he's not living as a pauper, that doesn't make him a bad man.

PATRICIA. He told me how he'd never set out to work in finance, how he'd wanted to be a gardener, for God's sake, a gardener? But he decided that the more money he earned, the more he'd be able to give away so he took a job at a bank and worked his way up. I mean, God I wanted to punch him.

SOFIA. Why?

PATRICIA. You don't get to do that.

SOFIA. What?

PATRICIA. Trick yourself into thinking all's square, when it's not.

SOFIA. So it'd be better if he didn't give anything?

PATRICIA. Those people who give nothing, they are what they are, they're not pretending to be better than that, they've got big houses and new cars and go skiing every weekend and to hell with the rest of us.

SOFIA. You think the world'd be a better place if we were all like that?

PATRICIA. It'd be more honest.

We can't face up to the way things are, that's our problem.

SOFIA. Who?

PATRICIA. People.

SOFIA. And how are things?

PATRICIA. Unfair.

> If Antonio had just told me I'm too old, that I have no experience they'd find useful, a suitable job will never come up, that he'll never be in touch, I could've handled that.

> If he said he gives away his money because he feels guilty about how privileged he is, how lucky he's been, how much he has, that'd be better.

SOFIA. Does it matter? If others benefit, does it really matter why he gives?

PATRICIA. The way he is, the

> He thinks he's fixed things when he hasn't.

> I don't want you thinking you've fixed anything. Giving your money away, all it means is we can't go to Daniel's wedding. It hasn't fixed anything.

Five

PATRICIA. I don't know what you want me to say Sofia.

SOFIA. Why Antonio?

PATRICIA. It's not personal.

> That's what you're always telling me, isn't it?

> Well it's not.

SOFIA. I find that a bit hard to believe.

PATRICIA. It is at first, but it gets easier.

SOFIA. Of all the people, hundreds and hundreds of people coming out of the office, he's the only one you spit at.

PATRICIA. I didn't spit at him.

SOFIA. One of you did.

PATRICIA. There's only one of me.

SOFIA. The protesters.

He's the only one. They targeted him.

PATRICIA. Targeted? One of the women just got carried away. He happened to be passing.

It's a dirty habit, but there's no permanent damage is there.

SOFIA. He's upset.

PATRICIA. Upset?

Well I hope he can get over it.

SOFIA. He said she looked like she wanted to kill him, as she did it.

PATRICIA. She was worked up.

It can't be the first time someone's looked at him like that. His line of work.

SOFIA. Why him?

PATRICIA. Why not him?

SOFIA. Because it's not about one individual.

PATRICIA. So she should spit at everyone?

Think it'd lose impact, as a gesture.

SOFIA. It's completely ridiculous to single him out, to blame one man, he's just part of a massive corporation, and he's not even right at the top, there are plenty of people with far more power than him, it makes no sense.

PATRICIA. What do our banners say?

Do they name Antonio? Do they single him out?

SOFIA. Your banners don't, no.

PATRICIA. So? One woman got carried away but in the grand scheme of things darling, a bit of spit, it's hardly the worst thing to happen.

SOFIA. Have you thought about how it looks for me, to have my mum standing outside protesting against the people I work for.

Against me too, I suppose.

PATRICIA. They don't know who I am.

SOFIA. Antonio does.

I do.

Have you thought about that?

PATRICIA. I'm not protesting against you. You're not responsible for this mess.

SOFIA. Neither's Antonio.

There are other banks. There are other places you could protest, if you wanted. But you choose my place of work. Why?

PATRICIA. This isn't the only place I've / been.

SOFIA. Why?

Pause.

PATRICIA. You marched, remember?

Before you got your job, you marched alongside Clara and the rest.

SOFIA. So what, I'm a traitor? I should skip work to march for jobs?

PATRICIA. No but you can understand what we're doing.

SOFIA. What Clara and the rest are doing, yes, but you never marched, before.

PATRICIA. I should've. I'm making up for it now.

Dad's all but given up, which is all the more reason to get out there and do something.

I'm allowed, same as anyone else.

SOFIA. Don't you think it's hypocritical?

Where do I get the money that pays for your mortgage?

Same people you condemn.

PATRICIA. I'm not condemning you Sofia, for going to work and doing your job.

SOFIA. Don't you feel like a fake? Standing here alongside all these protesters, knowing full well that bank is paying your mortgage.

PATRICIA. You're paying our mortgage, you, my daughter.

SOFIA. And who employs me?

PATRICIA. The more voices, Sofia, the more bodies, the stronger the movement. Maybe I am better off than some people here, because I happen to have a daughter in work, but that doesn't make me a fake, that doesn't mean I don't believe in what we're doing.

SOFIA. What are you doing?

Do you even know?

PATRICIA. We're sick of it. Of being taken for fools, of being patronised and sidelined, maybe we've had enough.

SOFIA. Don't undermine it then.

Don't get someone to spit in Antonio's face as if it's some high-minded political action when it's nothing more than

PATRICIA. Than what?

Pause.

I told you, that woman has nothing to do with me. How do you know she hasn't been spitting at others?

He told you it's just him, well how the hell would he know? As you say, he's nobody, why would she single him out?

Pause.

Invite him to dinner.

SOFIA. Antonio?

PATRICIA. I've got nothing against him, you'll see that.

SOFIA. The enemy? You're inviting the enemy for dinner?

PATRICIA. The saliva in his face, that had nothing to do with me.

Let me cook for him. I promise, I won't spit in his food.

SOFIA. You don't need to prove anything.

PATRICIA. It'd be nice.

SOFIA. It'd be weird.

PATRICIA. Why? You won't be alone, if that's what you mean, your father and I will be there.

SOFIA. That isn't what I meant.

PATRICIA. Invite his wife as well, of course.

SOFIA. I'm just his PA, it'd be

Odd.

PATRICIA. He agreed to meet me, which you've made clear is highly unusual.

He obviously thinks a lot of you.

SOFIA. Why? I mean really Mum, what's the point?

PATRICIA. You seem to think I'm against him.

SOFIA. I wonder where the hell I got that idea?

PATRICIA. Perhaps I just need to get to know him, as you do. I've only spoken to him for what, how long was our chat, fifteen minutes, I mean that's hardly enough time to form a fair opinion.

SOFIA. Why d'you need to have an opinion on him?

PATRICIA. It'd be good for your father too. To have some male company. Any company, really, he never leaves the house, Guido's the only one he sees.

SOFIA. I don't think Dad would fit in at the bank.

PATRICIA. It's not a ploy, Sofia, to get Dad work, or me for that matter.

It's just dinner. If you don't think he'd like it

SOFIA. I think the whole thing would be incredibly uncomfortable.

PATRICIA. Fine, it was just a suggestion.

I just think it's a shame these two parts of your life are so separate, so disconnected.

SOFIA. There are lots of things about your life Mum that I don't know. That I'll never know. People you've met, things you've done.

PATRICIA. Ask me anything.

SOFIA. Whatever I ask there'll always be things I don't know.

PATRICIA. And you don't care?

SOFIA. It's not that I don't care, that's just the nature of

PATRICIA. I care. As a mother, I want to know, I want to be part of your life.

SOFIA. You are a part of it.

PATRICIA. Because if I'm not even a part of your life, my own daughter, then what chance do I have of mattering to anyone, of having even the tiniest significance to anyone else?

SOFIA. You matter to

Lots of people. Dad for one. Me. And Daniel.

PATRICIA. On their honeymoon now.

SOFIA. You matter to lots of people.

Pause.

Look I'll ask him. I'll ask if he has the time. If it means that much to you.

PATRICIA. It does.

SOFIA. Then I'll ask.

Six

SOFIA. She doesn't even know these people.

PATRICIA. It's wonderful, isn't it.

SOFIA. She's barely looked at me.

PATRICIA. They're about to be evicted Sofia.

SOFIA. I know that.

PATRICIA. So what do you expect?

SOFIA. She has time to say hello.

PATRICIA. There's a lot going on.

SOFIA. One word, that's all I'm asking.

PATRICIA. Well go if you don't feel you're being appreciated enough, go.

SOFIA. I didn't know it was this bad.

PATRICIA. You were living here, you must've

SOFIA. She blames me, I know she does.

PATRICIA. She's angry.

SOFIA. At me. As if I'm the one that caused all this.

PATRICIA. She knows that's not true.

SOFIA. The money I was paying them to stay here, it was just about keeping them going but when I left

PATRICIA. You did the right thing.

SOFIA. I left them to this.

PATRICIA. Well it was us or them Sofia, you can't afford two mortgages. You did the right thing.

SOFIA. How can you say that when they're about to lose everything.

PATRICIA. Not everything.

SOFIA. Okay, just the home they've been paying for for twenty years.

PATRICIA. You're here now.

SOFIA. That's hardly enough.

PATRICIA. There's enough of us, they won't be able to evict them today, we'll win.

SOFIA. For a few weeks.

PATRICIA. If all we do is give those bastards one long throbbing headache, if it makes them think twice about what they're doing, that's something.

SOFIA. That's nothing, if they get evicted anyway.

Pause.

PATRICIA. I'm surprised Antonio let you come.

SOFIA. Let me? I'm not a slave.

PATRICIA. I didn't think the bank would be keen on having an employee attend an eviction protest.

SOFIA. Maybe I'm here on official business. Undercover, maybe I'm a spy.

PATRICIA. I wouldn't put it past them.

SOFIA. Maybe that's why Clara's not talking to me. Won't even risk a hello.

PATRICIA. Have you even tried to speak to her?

SOFIA. I lied to Antonio. Left work. I'm probably risking more than anyone else to be here but that's not enough apparently, she can't even acknowledge me.

PATRICIA. He doesn't know you're here?

SOFIA. I told him I was sick.

PATRICIA *smiles*.

Don't smile like that.

PATRICIA. Like what?

SOFIA. Like that.

PATRICIA. You don't look sick.

SOFIA. Seemed easier.

PATRICIA. This is important, he'd have understood wouldn't he?

Your best friend. Homeless.

What kind of human being wouldn't understand?

SOFIA. He's stressed.

PATRICIA. Well he must be busy if he doesn't even have time to come for a simple dinner.

Some people might've been offended, but I know how busy he is.

SOFIA. It's not just work, he's been

He's been getting these letters.

Threatening letters.

PATRICIA. Who from?

SOFIA. One of them threatened to burn his house down while he and his family are sleeping.

So now he can't sleep.

PATRICIA. Conscience about something.

SOFIA. He's scared.

PATRICIA. If you're completely innocent you brush it off.

SOFIA. Oh, you'd do that would you? You'd assume it was all just some misunderstanding.

PATRICIA. Who'd send me death threats? I'm nowhere near important enough.

Pause.

Has he involved the police?

SOFIA. He's got his wife and kids to stay with his parents for now. Says there's nothing the police can do anyway so

PATRICIA. He's right. All this technology we have, emails and things, they're clever at tracing that, but letters, they're harder to trace, I imagine. Not impossible of course, but he'd have to be very high-profile for them to bother.

SOFIA. Spent a lot of time thinking about it have you?

PATRICIA. He can't fire you. For missing half a day.

SOFIA. You better hope he can't.

Or we'll be doing this outside our own home, won't we.

Pause.

PATRICIA. Wouldn't be so bad.

SOFIA. What're you talking about?

PATRICIA. Well look at us.

SOFIA. What?

PATRICIA. You and me. Side by side. United.

SOFIA. We've got somewhere to go back to Mum. Not quite so romantic when it's your home on the line.

PATRICIA. When have we ever really done anything together?

SOFIA. My entire life.

PATRICIA. Not really. We'd do things for you, swimming lessons or whatever it was, and things for me, when I dragged you around old houses, but we've never really shared a common, an interest, have we.

SOFIA. I wouldn't call this an interest Mum.

PATRICIA. What would you call it?

SOFIA. Something I happen to be doing at this moment. A waste of time, probably.

If everything went back to normal, I wouldn't be standing outside Clara's house, like this, with you. Nothing personal but this isn't an interest.

PATRICIA. Perhaps that isn't the right word then, but

It's not a waste of time. Even if, even if they do end up losing the

Being here together like this, that's not a waste of time.

SOFIA. Together? Clara won't come anywhere near me.

PATRICIA. I'm not talking about Clara I'm talking about us. Mother and daughter. Side by side. How often does that happen?

Pause.

They've destroyed a lot of lives, / but they're

SOFIA. Who?

PATRICIA. But I've thought about what you said, Sofia. About seeing the potential in things. And you're right, there's plenty of potential in everything that's happening right now.

SOFIA. For what?

PATRICIA. To make something more of yourself. You're doing it, so what's stopping me? We're not so different.

Seven

PATRICIA. Are you nervous?

SOFIA. What do I have to be nervous about?

PATRICIA. Nothing, I just always, I always feel nervous before a funeral, I don't know why.

SOFIA. It's called grief Mum.

PATRICIA. No it's

I know what it is, I've buried enough people I loved Sofia and I know what I felt and on the day I felt nervous.

SOFIA. I didn't love him.

PATRICIA. You respected him. Liked him a lot.

SOFIA *nods*.

Pause.

Is everyone coming? The whole company, the whole

SOFIA. Just the people he worked with, the ones he knew personally.

PATRICIA. Can't drop everything I suppose, can they, things have to carry on.

Nice church. Old.

SOFIA. He wasn't even religious. He had his own mind, / he

PATRICIA. Don't tell the priest. Church like this, sure it's not easy getting a burial spot here. Highly prized, I'd say.

SOFIA. Amount of interest in his death, maybe they're reckoning on some tourism off the back of it.

Pause.

PATRICIA. Lot of people already, should we go in.

SOFIA. Don't see why you'd come to a funeral if you didn't know the person.

PATRICIA. Been so much about it, people feel like they did know him, I suppose.

SOFIA. They didn't.

PATRICIA. Not personally, no but

SOFIA. You only met him for fifteen minutes.

PATRICIA. Heard enough from you to feel like I'd known him my whole life.

SOFIA. Hardly your favourite person, was he.

PATRICIA. I'm here to support you more than / anything.

SOFIA. I'm fine.

PATRICIA. It's good to have someone with you.

SOFIA. I know people.

PATRICIA. Colleagues, yes, but

SOFIA. At least they knew him.

Least they think it'd be better if he was still here.

PATRICIA. You don't think I do?

SOFIA. I think a lot of people are very happy he's dead.

PATRICIA. Including me?

SOFIA. They think it solves something. As if it could.

They think it's some kind of penance that had to be paid. And now it has been, they think everything's going to be alright again. As if it could be. As if one man's death is any kind of payment.

Pause.

PATRICIA. You can see though, can't you, why people have made something of it. His death. The note he left.

SOFIA. Typed.

PATRICIA. You can see why people have read that as a

SOFIA. Anyone could've written it.

PATRICIA. You don't think he did?

SOFIA. Anyone could've.

PATRICIA. His handwriting was terrible, you said, it's not strange he'd type his note, is it? He wanted it to be understood.

SOFIA. Those weren't his words. He wasn't sorry for what he did, his role at the bank. He chose it, he could've done anything, if he'd had such doubts, such grave doubts, he could've done something else for money.

PATRICIA. You say that, but once you get used to a certain way of living it's hard, isn't it, it's hard to imagine something else.

We all suffer from that, the entire nation, that's our problem, isn't it.

SOFIA. We don't all kill ourselves.

Pause.

PATRICIA. You only saw him at work Sofia. I know you got on well, but that's just one side of him, he was probably very good at playing the / part, but

SOFIA. I don't know how she can stand it.

PATRICIA. Who?

SOFIA. His wife.

All these people, talking about him, when they didn't know him.

I don't think I can go in there, I don't know how I'll

They all want a part of him.

But they don't know the first thing about him, they don't even know that he wasn't the kind to kill himself.

PATRICIA. Is there a type?

SOFIA. He was passionate about helping people, however naive you might think that sounds, he / believed he could, that

PATRICIA. It's not naive, he has helped people.

SOFIA. His job gave him the means to do that, so there's no way he'd apologise for it, let alone

PATRICIA. It's not naive, Sofia. He has helped others.

The whole nation.

SOFIA. Death. That's not the kind of help he believed in.

PATRICIA. Can't you feel it? Can't you feel how people are different, since it happened, like someone's finally opened a window, let some air in.

SOFIA. Let some air in? Antonio's dead.

PATRICIA. If this is a war, us against them, the rich, the greedy, the ones that got us in this mess, we were losing, before, we were the only ones losing, but now

SOFIA. He slit his throat.

PATRICIA. Now people can see they're not unbreakable, that they have a conscience.

SOFIA. They? He. Antonio. Antonio had a conscience, not a guilty conscience, just a conscience.

He's not some representative of the banking community, the enemy, or however you see them.

PATRICIA. Not to you, no. But you knew him.

The rest of the country / see

SOFIA. The rest of the country see what they want to see. Whatever helps them believe they won't have to live like this much longer, that it might get better soon.

PATRICIA. It might get better now.

Isn't that all Antonio wanted?

SOFIA. Not all he wanted, no.

PATRICIA. However much of his salary he gave away in his lifetime he could never have hoped to achieve this level of

SOFIA. Bullshit.

PATRICIA. He wanted to be of use, didn't he. Well he has been.

SOFIA. So he's better off dead?

PATRICIA. No. But his death hasn't been in vain, that's it, that's what I'm trying to say.

Pause.

SOFIA. Why'd you want to be here?

PATRICIA. For you, I told you.

SOFIA. You hated him.

PATRICIA. Don't say that.

SOFIA. You said you wanted to punch him.

PATRICIA. Did I?

SOFIA. Yes.

PATRICIA. Well it's hardly

We all say things we / don't

SOFIA. You meant it.

PATRICIA. Well I didn't punch him, did I? What are you

SOFIA. You disliked him, no need to hide it, is there?

PATRICIA. The man's dead Sofia.

SOFIA. Exactly.

PATRICIA. It doesn't feel right to be

SOFIA. He's dead. He's not going to hear.

What, are you worried it might look suspicious?

PATRICIA. What?

SOFIA. Most of the country hated him. Not Antonio as such but the idea of him. Your instinctive dislike of him, that's only natural, you're entitled not to like him, that's fine, you can have your opinion.

An opinion's one thing.

PATRICIA. Whatever I thought of Antonio, and it feels wrong speaking ill of the dead, but

SOFIA. So you did hate him?

PATRICIA. Hate's a strong word.

SOFIA. But it's accurate isn't it?

PATRICIA. Does it matter what I thought?

SOFIA. Yeah, it does.

PATRICIA. Doesn't usually.

You seem to take it personally. Whatever I thought of him's got nothing to do with us, you and me.

SOFIA. How can they possibly think it's suicide when he was getting those notes?

How can they possibly believe that typed letter?

How can they ignore the fact Antonio would never have killed himself?

PATRICIA. You think he was murdered?

SOFIA. Yes I think he was murdered, I think it's perfectly clear he was and I have no idea why everyone's so fucking blind.

Pause.

PATRICIA. Threatening letters aren't uncommon Sofia.

His handwriting was bad so he typed his note.

And you said yourself he'd been stressed, stress does things to people, he wasn't in his right mind.

SOFIA. Of course you can explain it away if you want to.

They don't want it to be murder, that doesn't fit in with the whole 'penitent banker' story.

PATRICIA. They?

SOFIA. Everyone. The police, the media, the banking world, even his family, they don't want to believe he was slaughtered in their home, so that's it, suicide.

If it was murder then

We really would be at war.

PATRICIA. Would you rather that?

SOFIA. I'd rather he was still here.

PATRICIA. But since he's not, isn't it better that his death is the start of a recovery, rather than war?

SOFIA. Recovery? There's families of people who've committed suicide baying for more blood. They want a dead banker for every civilian who's killed themselves.

PATRICIA. They're in the minority.

SOFIA. What do they expect, obliging financial-sector workers to make voluntary suicides?

PATRICIA. They're angry, that's understandable. But they're a tiny proportion of the people.

This is a turning point.

You'll see.

In a way, he's lucky. Look how many people are here. His death means something. How many of us get to say that?

Eight

PATRICIA. Your father's working now, I don't see what all the fuss is about.

SOFIA. For now. He's freelance Mum, there's no guarantees.

PATRICIA. Guido said there's at least a year's work in it.

SOFIA. Well if Guido said then

PATRICIA. He's come through for us, hasn't he?

SOFIA. We need to take it slowly. No need to start planning extensions and new wardrobes and holidays and

PATRICIA. I want to see my nephew, that's all. Not too much to ask.

SOFIA. I just think you could let things settle down before booking a holiday.

PATRICIA. Family visit. Not a holiday, we won't be lounging on beaches all day drinking cocktails.

SOFIA. No it'll be work work work, won't it.

PATRICIA. We missed his wedding / Sofia.

SOFIA. I know.

PATRICIA. You said we'd go as soon as we could. Well, now we can.

SOFIA. You go then Mum. I know how much it means, you go.

PATRICIA. I'm not going without you, this is a family holiday, that's the whole point.

SOFIA. You said visit.

PATRICIA. Visit. Daniel wants to see all of us.

SOFIA. I can't just take time off / whenever

PATRICIA. You get holiday. They told you to take a few days over Antonio's funeral, but you didn't, so they owe you, you're entitled to this.

SOFIA. I'm not entitled to anything.

PATRICIA. You work hard, you've taken no time off since you've been here.

SOFIA. It doesn't look good if you're always / taking

PATRICIA. I'm only talking a week Sofia. Five days.

I think you've proved yourself by now. You're not on probation or anything are you?

SOFIA. Mr Fisher doesn't really know me.

PATRICIA. You do your job, what else does he need to know?

SOFIA. Nothing, apparently.

I don't know if he's trying to be the opposite of Antonio, but I couldn't even tell you if he's married. Or where he's from.

PATRICIA. Keeps things professional, no harm in that.

SOFIA. His handwriting's so perfect it's creepy.

PATRICIA. Then no one will have trouble reading it, will they. They'll manage without you.

I'd like to spend some proper time with my daughter, not just these rushed lunchtime meetings when you've always got to get back before you've even sat down.

It's not such a terrible thing to want, is it?

SOFIA. No one said it's terrible, it's a nice idea.

PATRICIA. That's settled then. I'll go to the agent this afternoon.

SOFIA. It just doesn't feel right to be

PATRICIA. All that's happened, with Antonio, doesn't it make you want to seize the moment, enjoy the time we have?

SOFIA. He wasn't hit by a bus Mum, it wasn't some freak accident.

PATRICIA. No but

Things are getting better, look around, they're on the up, can't we celebrate that a little? Breathe a little sigh of relief even.

SOFIA. Bit early for that.

PATRICIA. We're not doing badly. Dad back in work, you in your job.

SOFIA. As long as we're alright.

PATRICIA. It's not just us. You helped Clara get an interview.

SOFIA. It's just an interview.

PATRICIA. It's a chance at least.

SOFIA. I can't just forget.

PATRICIA. Forget what?

SOFIA. What he tried to do. The way he lived.

PATRICIA. What about it?

SOFIA. I have a responsibility.

PATRICIA. Yes, you do. To your family. To yourself.

SOFIA. To other people too.

PATRICIA. You saw his house Sofia.

I think you're in danger of

When someone dies it's easy to paint them as something other than they were.

SOFIA *shakes her head.*

He wasn't a saint, and what did you really know about him?

SOFIA. So what? So what if he didn't give every cent he had.

PATRICIA. There must've been something going on Sofia, you don't kill yourself unless / there's some

SOFIA. Mr Fisher couldn't give a shit. He probably doesn't even know my name.

PATRICIA. You can't have a special bond with everyone.

SOFIA. If he can't even be bothered to learn my name, someone he sees every day, what does that say about his attitude in general?

PATRICIA. He's not a people person.

Look there aren't many people who'll learn your name, even fewer who'll remember it.

You don't matter to many people at all. Neither do I. That's the truth of it. That's why, family, friends, we're the ones you should be spending time with, not worrying about someone the other side of the world you'll never meet, or what a dead man you barely knew would've done.

SOFIA. I knew him.

PATRICIA. I can't help but wonder if

When, not if, when

When I'm gone if you'll be anywhere near as affected by that.

SOFIA. What kind of thing to say is that?

PATRICIA *shrugs.*

Pause.

PATRICIA. What harm would a holiday do? Who would it hurt?

Nine

SOFIA. Look at it properly.

PATRICIA. Very nice.

SOFIA. You haven't even looked at it.

PATRICIA. It's a watch, I've seen watches.

SOFIA. She didn't have to get me anything.

PATRICIA. Well you did help her.

SOFIA. Of course I'm going to help her.

PATRICIA. We all helped them. Everyone who stood outside at that protest, saved their house, she going to buy us all watches?

SOFIA. It wasn't for the protest, it was / for the

PATRICIA. I know it was for the job Sofia.

SOFIA. It's more of a peace offering I think, it's not / like I

PATRICIA. We got you a watch.

SOFIA. And I've worn it every day, haven't I?

PATRICIA. Can't wear two.

SOFIA. Not at the same time, no, but different occasions, doesn't hurt / to have two.

PATRICIA. You could take it back I suppose.

SOFIA. Why would I do that?

PATRICIA. Choose something else, where did she get it?

SOFIA. I don't want something else.

PATRICIA. Depends where she got it I suppose, be awkward, if it's not authentic, / if it's

SOFIA. It's not a fake and I'm not taking it back.

PATRICIA. Fine.

SOFIA. I like it. I don't want to take it back.

PATRICIA. No.

SOFIA. What kind of message would that send?

PATRICIA. Message?

SOFIA. It's an important

PATRICIA. What?

SOFIA. Thing.

Between Clara and me, like we're friends again, like we're back to normal.

PATRICIA. Doesn't normally buy you watches does she?

SOFIA. We're talking, like normal. There's no weird tension in the air, it's nice.

PATRICIA. Doesn't she know you've already got a watch?

SOFIA. She wasn't trying to replace yours Mum, it's just a nice thing to give someone, isn't it.

PATRICIA *nods*.

You were right.

PATRICIA. That'd be a first.

SOFIA. When you said things are getting better.

PATRICIA. I didn't mean between you and Clara.

SOFIA. I know that, but generally they are.

PATRICIA. A friendship shouldn't depend on the state of the economy.

SOFIA. It doesn't.

PATRICIA. You helped before, paid rent on a sofa, put in a good word at work when you could, but she wouldn't even look at you then.

SOFIA. She had a lot going on.

PATRICIA. Excuses.

SOFIA. She was off with me, you're right.

PATRICIA. More than that.

SOFIA. She was. But she admits it and we've been friends long enough / that

PATRICIA. You're too nice.

SOFIA. Do you know what she said?

She said Antonio changed her mind.

PATRICIA. About what?

SOFIA. She admits she was probably a bit judgemental, a bit you know self-righteous about banks and my job, but actually Antonio made her think.

PATRICIA. Antonio?

SOFIA. And if she was affected others must've been too, which is what you said from the start.

PATRICIA. What did I say?

SOFIA. That his death could achieve more good than anything else he could've done, which I didn't want to believe and obviously I wish he hadn't done what he did but it has had an impact, things are improving, the worst is behind us.

People need something big to make them think in a different way and Antonio knew that. It's the only reason he would've taken such an extreme measure. He wanted to matter, he wanted to help, and Clara's proof that he has.

She was bitter, she'll admit that now, hard not to be, the entire nation was. She needed someone to pay, take responsibility and Antonio did that.

And if she sees it that way, others will too. You were right.

At the time, it felt like he'd betrayed me, I couldn't understand, but I see it now.

There's no way I'd ever change this watch. It's from Clara, but it feels like it's from Antonio really.

PATRICIA. It wasn't suicide.

You were right. You didn't think it was, and you were right, he wasn't the type.

They cut his throat.

SOFIA. Who?

PATRICIA. That doesn't matter.

SOFIA. What are you talking about?

PATRICIA. They weren't after fame.

SOFIA. Who?

PATRICIA. We weren't after medals. Just a solution. And we got that.

SOFIA. We, now?

PATRICIA. I didn't cut his throat, but I played my part.

SOFIA. And what was that exactly?

PATRICIA. I found him.

SOFIA. Right.

PATRICIA. You don't think I was involved?

SOFIA. Involved in what?

PATRICIA. His murder.

SOFIA. I don't know what the hell you're talking about.

PATRICIA. It's quite simple.

SOFIA. He killed himself.

PATRICIA *shakes her head.*

PATRICIA. Wasn't the type.

SOFIA. But you're definitely the murdering kind I suppose.

PATRICIA. It's not that hard.

SOFIA. Do it a lot do you?

PATRICIA. No, first time, but it was very easy actually. Not that I plan to do it again.

SOFIA. Course not.

PATRICIA. We had an objective, and that was achieved so

SOFIA. Which was?

PATRICIA. Help.

SOFIA. That's it? That's the grand manifesto?

PATRICIA. Pretty much. And we achieved that, as you were saying.

SOFIA. I was saying things were improving.

PATRICIA. Which was our objective.

Pause.

SOFIA. Who were you working with then?

PATRICIA. A small group of activists.

SOFIA. Extremists?

PATRICIA. None of us want anything very extreme.

SOFIA. But you'll murder to get it so that's kind of extreme.

PATRICIA. Only one man.

Only takes one, if you choose wisely.

SOFIA. And that's where you came in?

PATRICIA *nods.*

PATRICIA. I knew he was the right one.

SOFIA. And how was that? Because I liked him? Because of all the good things I said about him, you figured he had to go.

PATRICIA. I don't know the exact moment I decided, but you helped.

SOFIA. Oh I'm an accomplice now, am I?

PATRICIA. Where he worked, where he lived, where he went for drinks. Couldn't have done it without you. You should be proud.

SOFIA. Should I?

PATRICIA. We did more to help Spain than the politicians and EU bureaucrats combined. We understood what the people wanted and we gave it to them.

SOFIA. And what's that?

PATRICIA. Blood.

But not too much. Just enough.

SOFIA. Just one man?

PATRICIA. If it's the right one, that's enough.

SOFIA. And that's where you came in.

PATRICIA. You don't have to believe me.

SOFIA. Would you like me to?

PATRICIA. It worked. That's all I need to know.

Pause.

SOFIA. So they broke into his house, is that right? And cut his throat. And made it look like suicide.

PATRICIA. You'd told me how his wife and kids were staying elsewhere. No one was around.

And I told them it'd be fine to type the note. How his handwriting was notoriously bad.

You can't be squeamish.

You were just saying his death achieved more good than anything else he could've done.

SOFIA. I said I wished he hadn't done it.

PATRICIA. Because you're squeamish.

SOFIA. Because I wish he wasn't dead. If I had the choice, if it was down to me, he'd still be here.

PATRICIA. Things are improving, you said it yourself.

SOFIA. They'd be improving if he was still here.

PATRICIA *shakes her head.*

They would.

PATRICIA. Well we can't prove it now, but I disagree.

Things would be the same as they were.

Your father at home.

Clara ignoring you.

The country at a standstill, everyone stuck, no one able to get past the bitterness.

The right people never get the credit, and I don't expect praise, or national recognition, or even a thanks.

SOFIA. That's probably just as well.

PATRICIA. The way we did it, Antonio looks like the saviour. He'll be remembered, he'll be the one they talk about in textbooks, the turning point. And for that reason I can live with myself.

SOFIA. You can stop now, whatever this is.

PATRICIA. Why would I lie?

SOFIA. I have no idea.

PATRICIA. I wouldn't.

Pause.

I knew Antonio would never give me a job. You knew that too. But you got me in.

SOFIA. You said you'd wait outside all night, you didn't give me much choice.

PATRICIA. You got me access.

SOFIA. You refused to leave.

You can't possibly think I was a willing accomplice because I introduced you.

And you can't possibly expect me to believe that someone who's attended two or three protests in her life somehow has connections to an extremist terrorist cell.

PATRICIA. They're not terrorists. We only murdered one man.

SOFIA. And you can't possibly expect me to believe that.

PATRICIA. I did what you told me to do Sofia, I dared to take a risk.

SOFIA. A risk?

PATRICIA. I had the courage of my convictions.

SOFIA. What convictions?

PATRICIA. My beliefs. You don't think I have beliefs?

SOFIA. Not ones you'd kill someone over, no.

PATRICIA. And what convictions do you have?

SOFIA. I don't know, don't kill people. Don't tell people you have when you haven't. Don't act like it'd be no big thing.

Simple stuff like that.

PATRICIA. I won't be telling anyone else.

SOFIA. Well that's something.

PATRICIA. This is between us.

SOFIA. I think that's a good idea, you start saying stuff like this, God knows.

PATRICIA. Just us.

SOFIA. Good.

PATRICIA. It's something I want us to share.

SOFIA. Most mothers and daughters share dresses. Or gossip. Or even genetic defects, but no, we have to share this.

PATRICIA. When I die

SOFIA. Oh for God's sake Mum.

PATRICIA. When I do, you'll know what your inheritance is. What I did for you.

SOFIA. I'd rather have jewellery.

PATRICIA. You'll know I had convictions and I had the courage of them.

SOFIA. I'll know you had a fucked-up imagination.

PATRICIA. You'll be grateful.

That we shared this thing that not even your father was part of. When you sit in that pew at my funeral, you'll hold on to this shared thing of ours and it'll mean something then. And when someone stands up and tries to cobble together some kind of significance, tries to talk about me as if I meant something, you'll know that I did. You'll / know

SOFIA. Mum, you do mean

PATRICIA. You'll know they're missing the most important bit, but it won't matter, because you know it, and that's all that matters.

Ten

SOFIA. They're saying Antonio might've been murdered.

PATRICIA. He was. I told you that. Coffee?

SOFIA. Reopening the investigation. How did you know?

PATRICIA. I was part of it.

SOFIA. Did you read it somewhere? A conspiracy-theory website, some forum, is that where you got it?

PATRICIA. I wouldn't even know how they worked.

SOFIA. Then where did you hear it?

PATRICIA. I didn't have to hear it, I was part of it.

SOFIA. If you say things like that, if you

Now's not the time to be saying stuff like that.

PATRICIA. I told you, I'd only say it to you. It's ours.

SOFIA. How did you know?

PATRICIA. I was involved Sofia.

SOFIA. Aren't you worried then?

PATRICIA. Who's going to come after me? I'm not on anybody's radar. And anyway, I wasn't the one to cut his throat.

SOFIA. That won't matter, if you were involved.

PATRICIA. If?

    If you don't believe me, what are you getting so upset about?

SOFIA. Antonio might've been murdered.

PATRICIA. He was.

SOFIA. So maybe that's why I'm upset.

PATRICIA. They won't catch anyone.

SOFIA. That's comforting.

PATRICIA. Case like this they have to look like they've been thorough, that's all this is. It won't come to anything. We're a bunch of nobodies. Never been in trouble before. They won't find anything. Have you had something to eat?

SOFIA. I'm not a nobody, I'm his PA, they'll question me, won't they, they'll question me and I'll have to go through it all again.

PATRICIA. What are you worried about?

SOFIA. Maybe I don't want to go through it all again.

    It's bad enough I have to read Antonio's name practically every day in some article or other, now they're going to rake over it, it'll be all anyone talks about for months, why can't people / just let it

PATRICIA. Used to like talking about him. All you could do.

SOFIA. Well now I don't, now I just want to get on with things, we all should.

PATRICIA. I agree.

SOFIA. It's not going to look good that I was at that eviction protest is it.

PATRICIA. Not a crime.

SOFIA. Day he died, bit

PATRICIA. You weren't doing anything wrong. She's your best friend, you had to be there.

SOFIA. Why can't we all just

PATRICIA. Forget about it?

SOFIA. Not forget about it, but

If he's been murdered I want them to find the bastards, and I'll do everything I can to help.

PATRICIA *nods*.

Don't nod like that.

PATRICIA. Like what?

SOFIA. I will. If he was murdered

PATRICIA. He was.

SOFIA. Stop saying that.

PATRICIA. It's true.

SOFIA. I'll tell them everything I know.

PATRICIA. Even about me?

SOFIA. Things that will help them, not the delusional mutterings of a

PATRICIA. Of a?

I don't think I mutter, I think I speak quite clearly.

So you'll tell them how you went to his house when his wife was away, things like that, helpful things.

SOFIA. He'd left his keys at the office. You drove me over, you saw, I just gave him the keys and we left.

PATRICIA. Yes, I did. I did drive you over.

SOFIA. Why would they need to know that? That's not the kind of thing that's going to be helpful.

It's done, he's dead, I don't see the point in going back over any of it.

It's just picking at a scab, that's all this is.

PATRICIA. Let them. I'm not worried.

SOFIA. Why should you be?

Pause.

They'd yawn in my face if I started reeling off details.

PATRICIA. My mum and I drove to his house once to drop off his keys.

SOFIA. I showed my mum around the office one night.

PATRICIA. I attended an eviction protest on company time.

SOFIA. My mum thought I fucked Antonio to get the job.

My mum says she did it.

PATRICIA. I did.

Silence.

Your father's contract's been extended another year.

He's good at what he does, works hard, why wouldn't they want to keep him on.

Just happy he's back out there again, doing what he loves.

We're lucky.

SOFIA. Luck?

PATRICIA. Luckier than most.

SOFIA. Make your own luck, don't you?

PATRICIA. Well

All got to do our bit I suppose.

Should be down on our knees really. Thanking whoever's up there.

SOFIA. You're the one

PATRICIA. Maybe Antonio's looking out for us.

SOFIA. You're the one playing God.

You think you've fixed things but

Pause.

I want you to know

PATRICIA. Yes?

SOFIA. I want you to know that I miss him.

PATRICIA. I do know that.

SOFIA. All the time.

PATRICIA. Natural.

But you must find comfort in how much good has come from his death.

You must find some comfort in that?

Sofia?

Silence.

SOFIA. I'm late for work.

A Nick Hern Book

Merit first published in Great Britain in 2015 by Nick Hern Books Limited,
The Glasshouse, 49a Goldhawk Road, London W12 8QP

This revised edition published 2016

Merit copyright © 2015, 2016 Alexandra Wood

Alexandra Wood has asserted her moral right to be identified as the author of
this work

Cover image: © www.istockphoto.com/franckreporter

Designed and typeset by Nick Hern Books, London
Printed in Great Britain by Mimeo Ltd, Huntingdon, Cambridgeshire
PE29 6XX

A CIP catalogue record for this book is available from the British Library

ISBN 978 1 84842 557 6

Woodland
CARBON
www.woodlandcarbon.co.uk
NICK HERN BOOKS
Printed on Carbon Captured paper

www.nickhernbooks.co.uk

facebook.com/nickhernbooks

twitter.com/nickhernbooks